DANIEL OLAWANDE

STAYING HOT

MAINTAINING THE FIRE ON YOUR ALTAR

CONTENTS

DEDICATION

I dedicate the book the Almighty God, my father my maker, to my Lord Jesus Christ who is my savior and the one who baptizes with fire and the Holy spirit my senior partner, my companion, my friend, my inspiration, my utterance and my anointing.

ACKNOWLEDGMENTS

A tree cannot make a forest, a wise man once said, if you are not going far, go alone but if you are going very far, go with other people.

I want to appreciate God for the gift of men and women around me, those who work tirelessly to ensure this book become a reality.

First and foremost is my dearly beloved beautiful wife Oluwanifemi Olawande, thanks for the push every time, you are a gift sent from God.

I want to appreciate my boss, Pastor Tunji Adeboyejo who is also my publisher, thanks for always doing a good job and making it easy for me to be an author.

I sincerely appreciate all my team members that worked on this book, Naomi David Adeola, Fabian George, Omotayo Olusanya, Oluwaseyi Olubunmi, thank you all.

Lastly, I want to specially appreciate my editor, Osham Precious, the Lord bless you. Thank you so much, this piece is a success because you all did a good job.

God bless you all

INTRODUCTION

Romans 12:11, International Standard Version, "Never be lazy in showing such devotion. Be on fire with the Spirit. Serve the Lord."

Catching the fire is ok but staying hot, staying on fire is better. If you check the scriptures in the new testament you will see a continual in filling experience with the Apostles, it didn't end on the day of Pentecost, the kept moving from one level of fire to the other.

In the things of the Spirit, you cant be in the middle, you can't be lukewarm, it's either you are hot or you are cold.

One of the major questions in the heart of everyone that receives something precious from someone important is how do I keep this?, so also everyone that gets fire from the Lord will also be concerned about how to stay hot and even increase the fire.

This book is a destiny manual explained In the simplest form to enable you understand how to remain hot and even increase your fire.

It's so practical and filled with step by step details of how to maintain a glowing life.

Feed on this book, digest it, read it over and over again and you will discover that your fire will never go out forever in Jesus name.

I pray for you, as you read this book a fresh fire will rest upon your altar in the name of Jesus and you will burn for God forever in the name of Jesus.

UNDERSTANDING THE CONCEPT OF AN ALTAR

An altar can be simply defined as a structure or an elevated platform upon which offerings such as sacrifices are continually made for religious purposes irrespective of its location.

To establish a foundational understanding of an altar, two conditions must be ascertained:

1. An altar must be an elevated platform: The altar is a hallowed territory, a secluded and consecrated place of worship.

2. Sacrifices must be made on an altar: The making of a sacrifice on an elevated structure activates the altar.

Continual sacrifices keep the altar activated and when there are no more sacrifices, it becomes nothing but a used structure.

If you cannot find these two conditions in place, then it is not an altar. With this basic understanding, the spiritual heart can be an altar, as long as it is elevated for worship and continual sacrifices are made unto God, meaning our lives and entire being are dedicated unto God for worship.

THE DESIRE FOR ALTARS

Beloved, there is a deep desire on the inside of man that was implanted by God, a desire for an altar where sacrifices are consistently made.

It is evident that before the law was given, there was an innate desire in man to make sacrifices on an elevated platform. It's a desire for worship.

Let's study some examples:

Cain and Abel
And Adam knew Eve, his wife; and she conceived, and bare Cain, and said, I have gotten a man from the Lord. And she again bare his brother Abel. And Abel was a keeper of sheep, but Cain was a tiller of the ground. And in process of time it came to pass, that Cain brought of the fruit of the ground an offering unto the Lord. And Abel, he also

brought of the firstlings of his flock and of the fat thereof. And the Lord had respect unto Abel and to his offering: But unto Cain and to his offering he had not respect. And Cain was very wroth, and his countenance fell. And the Lord said unto Cain, Why art thou wroth? and why is thy countenance fallen? If thou doest well, shalt thou not be accepted? and if thou doest not well, sin lieth at the door. And unto thee shall be his desire, and thou shalt rule over him.
Genesis 4: 1-7 KJV

The above scripture showed us the very first altar raised to offer sacrifices unto God just after the fall of man in the Garden of Eden. Two brothers came together and were inspired to offer sacrifices unto God, out of the fruits of their labour.

One offered an animal out of his flock, the other offered out of the fruits of the ground. They elevated a platform and offered their sacrifices on it without any prior law or instruction as to how to get it done. This was the first example and illustration of altars and sacrifices in the Bible.

Noah

There is another example of a man called Noah who also raised an altar to offer sacrifices unto

God after the flood.

And Noah builded an altar unto the Lord; and took of every clean beast, and of every clean fowl, and offered burnt offerings on the altar. And the Lord smelled a sweet savour; and the Lord said in his heart, I will not again curse the ground any more for man's sake; for the imagination of man's heart is evil from his youth; neither will I again smite any more every thing living, as I have done. Genesis 8: 20-21 KJV

The question to ask here is who instructed him? Was there ever a time God commanded him to offer sacrifices unto Him?

Did God command Cain and Abel to offer sacrifices? The answer to all these questions is NO. There is just a natural desire in man to worship and raise altars.

Abraham
There was another man called Abraham. He also raised an altar unto God. Every man in the old testament that had something to do with God raised an altar unto God.

Abraham raised altars unto the Lord as we can find in the following scriptures:

And the Lord appeared unto Abram, and said, Unto thy seed will I give this land: and there builded he an altar unto the Lord, who appeared unto him Genesis 12:7 KJV

Then Abram removed his tent, and came and dwelt in the plain of Mamre, which is in Hebron, and built there an altar unto the Lord. Genesis 13:18 KJV

Moses
An altar of earth thou shalt make unto me, and shalt sacrifice thereon thy burnt offerings, and thy peace offerings, thy sheep, and thine oxen: in all places where I record my name I will come unto thee, and I will bless thee. And if thou wilt make me an altar of stone, thou shalt not build it of hewn stone: for if thou lift up thy tool upon it, thou hast polluted it. Neither shalt thou go up by steps unto mine altar, that thy nakedness be not discovered thereon. Exodus 20:24 -26 KJV

Moses built the altar according to the pattern that was revealed to him. The earthly buildings of the temple was a representation of what was in

ACTIVITIES ON THE ALTAR

The altar is a place to meet with God, a place of sacrifice. Sacrifices are made on the altar unto God because He has placed His name on the altar. The altar is also a place where we minister to the Lord.

'An altar of earth thou shalt make unto me, and shalt sacrifice thereon thy burnt offerings, and thy peace offerings, thy sheep, and thine oxen: in all places where I record my name I will come unto thee, and I will bless thee. ' Exodus 20:24 KJV

'and they shall be upon Aaron, and upon his sons, when they come in unto the tabernacle of the congregation, or when they come near unto the altar to minister in the holy place; that they bear not iniquity, and die: it shall be a statute for ever unto him and his seed after him.'
Exodus 28:43 KJV

So many people come to the presence of God with the sole purpose of being ministered unto alone. But we are to come to God's presence to minister unto God first, before being ministered unto.

Our worship, prayers, word declaration, praises are channels of ministration unto God. They are the sacrifices we make on the altar unto the Lord.

'By him therefore let us offer the sacrifice of praise to God continually, that is, the fruit of our lips giving thanks to his name.'

Hebrews 13:15 KJV

Our praise is a sacrifice from our lips. An altar is ineffective without sacrifices. Let us x-ray the altar and the activities that go on there.

'And the fire upon the altar shall be burning in it; it shall not be put out: and the priest shall burn wood on it every morning, and lay the burnt offering in order upon it; and he shall burn thereon the fat of the peace offerings. The fire shall ever be burning upon the altar; it shall never go out.'

Leviticus 6:12-13 KJV

HERE ARE SOME DISCOVERIES FROM THE SCRIPTURE ABOVE:

The fire must be burning on the altar regularly. The spiritual fire that should burn on the altar on a daily basis is not literal fire, but it could be explained as fresh love for God, fervency, consistency, passion for the things of the spirit, more hunger and thirst for the presence and power of God.

There must be sacrifice on the altar. If the fire must continue to burn and not go out, then the sacrifice must not finish. Rather the sacrifices must increase.

In the old testament, we see sacrifices being made on the altar with animals. They used the blood of animals. But as new testament believers, we are not to do that. Rather, the scripture clearly points out to us that we are now the sacrifice. We are to present our bodies as living sacrifices unto God.

So, if there should be sacrifice on the altar regularly and the scripture points to the fact that we should present our bodies as living sacrifices, it means, your body should be on the altar consistently, burning for the Lord.

You might ask, "What kind of burning? Am I going to be destroyed?" No no. To present your body as a living sacrifice means to surrender yourself and the appetites of the body.

It means your body is no more in charge, no longer in control and has been submitted under control of the Lord of the altar.

Under the old covenant, God accepted the sacrifices of dead animals. But in the new covenant, because of Christ's ultimate sacrifice, the sacrifices in the old testament are no longer acceptable and are no longer in effect.

'But Christ being come an high priest of good things to come, by a greater and more perfect tabernacle, not made with hands, that is to say, not of this building; neither by the blood of goats and calves, but by his own blood he entered in once into the holy place, having obtained eternal redemption for us.

For if the blood of bulls and of goats, and the ashes of an heifer sprinkling the unclean, sanctifieth to the purifying of the flesh: how much more shall the blood of Christ, who through the eternal Spirit offered himself without spot to God, purge your conscience from dead works to serve the living God?'

Hebrews 9:11-14 KJV

From the above scriptures, we see that the sacrifices of the old covenant have been done away with as a result of Christ's Ultimate Sacrifice via his death.

The only acceptable sacrifice now is to completely offer ourselves to the Lord. Now, if we are expected to also present ourselves as sacrifices, we are to take the pathway of death, just like Jesus.

Looking at the scripture below carefully:

'I beseech you therefore, brethren, by the mercies of God, that you present your bodies a living sacrifice, holy, acceptable to God, which is your reasonable service. '

Romans: 12:2 KJV

We will discover that the sacrifice here is a living sacrifice. Normally, before an animal can be called a sacrifice, it has to be killed before it can be butchered and presented on the altar. But in our own case, we are to be living sacrifices, i.e., we are alive yet sacrificed. This is a tough one.

The only way to be a living sacrifice is to be alive physically but dead to the works and dictates of the flesh. This means our bodies are no longer in control, our bodies have become subdued, placed under and the desires and appetites of the body are put under check.

We can't effectively talk about the concept of being a sacrifice without talking about death. Even though God is calling us into becoming a living sacrifice, this can only open after we have died to something.

To be an effective living sacrifice
we have to die.

Death is the pathway to life. What are the things we are to die to? To be a sacrifice, the first thing to die to is self. When a man dies to self. It means he is no longer in the picture.

The self ceases to exist. Philosophy says live for self but God says die to self.

'I am crucified with Christ: nevertheless I live; yet not I, but Christ liveth in me: and the life which I now live in the flesh I live by the faith of the Son of God, who loved me, and gave himself for me.'

Galatians 2:20 KJV

Apostle Paul said in the above scripture that it is no longer him that lives because he is dead. He basically said, "I am crucified with Christ, I am dead to myself and my desires."

When a man is dead to self, it means he is dead to his wants and desires, that sense of self-centeredness and selfishness. His heart desires only the will of God. A man that is dead to self is a man that has lost himself in God. He is now living according to the dictates of Yeshua.

'For whosoever will save his life shall lose it: and whosoever will lose his life for my sake shall find it.'

Matthew 16:25 KJV

We can now pay attention to the needs and cares of others when we are no longer obsessed with ourselves or our own interests. See this manifested in the life of the Apostle Paul in 1 Corinthians 9:27.

Several versions of the scripture explain this verse in an illustrative manner:

NIV: 'No, I strike a blow to my body and make it my slave so that after I have preached to others, I myself will not be disqualified for the prize.'

NLT: 'I discipline my body like an athlete, training it to do what it should. Otherwise, I fear that after preaching to others I myself might be disqualified.'

Berean Study Bible: 'No, I discipline my body and make it my slave, so that after I have preached to others, I myself will not be disqualified.'

Goodnews: 'I harden my body with blows and bring it under complete control, to keep myself from being disqualified after having called others to the contest.'

KJV: 'but I keep under my body, and bring it into subjection: lest that by any means, when I have preached to others, I myself should be a castaway.'

TPT: 'but I train like a champion athlete. I subdue my body and get it under my control, so that after preaching the good news to others I myself won't be disqualified.'

AMP: 'But [like a boxer] I strictly discipline my body and make it my slave, so that, after I have preached [the gospel] to others, I myself will not somehow be disqualified [as unfit for service].'

From the versions above, we will discover that to present your body as a living sacrifice means to submit your body for control.

Wood: In case there is sacrifice and the fire is going down, there is a need for the priest to go and look for wood to fuel the fire. When the wood is placed inside the fire, the priest has to blow up the fire and fan the flames, so that the wood can keep burning.

The wood is the fuel. It is the fuel that enables the fire to keep burning without going out. So the work of the priest is to add fuel to the fire daily to ensure it's always burning.

What are the kinds of woods (fuel) that must be added to the fire on the altar?

The wood of the word: The priest is supposed to burn the wood of the word of God daily upon the altar.

'Is not my word like as a fire? saith the Lord; and like a hammer that breaketh the rock in pieces?'

Jeremiah 23:29 KJV

The word of God is a daily diet to champions. When Jesus was tempted by the devil, he simply responded by saying in **Matthew 4:4 KJV, *"But he answered and said, It is written, Man shall not live by bread alone, but by every word that proceedeth out of the mouth of God."***

The more the word intake the more the fire level. Any man that will matter in the things of God is a man that will consistently feed on the word of God.

The wood of a prayer life: The priest should not just pray but he should have a life of prayer, a life that is emitting prayers. I like The Passion Translation rendition of *1 Thessalonians 5:17*, *"Make your life a prayer."*

The wood of meditation on the word of God: As the priest begins to meditate on the word of God, he begins to add fuel to the fire burning on the altar of his heart. The deeper the meditation, the more the fire.

'My heart burned with a fire within me, and my thoughts eventually boiled over until they finally came rolling out of my mouth:'

Psalms 39:3-4 TPT

The wood of flaming associations: The kind of company one keeps determines the fire level. The priest is supposed to keep company with flaming minds.

'As one piece of iron sharpens another, so friends keep each other sharp. '

Proverbs 27:17 ERV

The wood of fellowship: In order to maintain and increase the fire, the priest needs to burn the wood by fellowshipping with other brethren. The Bible never encourages isolation from the brethren; rather it encourages us not to forsake the gathering of one another.

'Not forsaking our meeting together [as believers for worship and instruction], as is the habit of some, but encouraging one another; and all the more [faithfully] as you see the day [of Christ's return] approaching. '

Hebrews 10:25 AMP

The wood of consistency: Anyone that will carry the fire of God in a generation will only be able to achieve that on the strength of his consistency in putting all the above woods in the fire daily. Consistency is a major secret of greatness.

The priest: The priest is the person who has the responsibility of blowing up the fire to ensure it doesn't go out. He burns wood on the altar regularly, he monitors the altar.

'And from Jesus Christ, the faithful witness, the firstborn from the dead, and the ruler over the kings of the earth. To Him who loved us and washed us from our sins in His own blood, and has made us kings and priests to His God and Father, to Him be glory and dominion forever and ever. Amen.'

Revelation 1:5-6 KJV

Thank God for the revelation in the scriptures. The priest is YOU. The scripture above says Christ had made you a king and priest unto God, meaning this is your present reality, not that he will make you a king and priest tomorrow.

The scripture makes it clear that king and priest is your present identity now because of what Christ has done.

'But you are a chosen generation, a royal priesthood, a holy nation, His own special people, that you may proclaim the praises of Him who called you out of darkness into His marvelous light;'

I Peter 2:9 KJV

The scripture above further elucidates your status as a priest, but not just any priest, a royal (king) priest.

Remember, the altar is the place to minister unto the Lord, and Christ has made us priests unto God.

So I am the priest, you are the priest. In Leviticus 6:12, we see that the priest is to burn wood on the altar daily. So it means you are to burn wood on your own altar daily as a priest.

Read through this scripture again and put your name where you find 'the priest'.

'And the fire upon the altar shall be burning in it; it shall not be put out: and the priest shall burn wood on it every morning, and lay the burnt offering in order upon it; and he shall burn thereon the fat of the peace offerings.'

Leviticus 6:12 KJV

You are the priest! So what are you supposed to do? You are expected to put wood every morning on your altar. Place sacrifices on your altar.

I know you would begin to ask yourself a question right now, "Do I have an altar? What is the sacrifice to place on my altar?" Let us look into the word. Your answers are not far-fetched.

The Sacrifice
'I beseech you therefore, brethren, by the mercies of God, that ye present your bodies a living sacrifice, holy acceptable unto God, which is your reasonable service.'

Romans 12:1 KJV

From the scripture above, it is therefore established that your body is the sacrifice to be placed on the altar and you are the priest. Glory to God!

WHERE IS YOUR ALTAR?
We have established that an altar is an elevated platform where sacrifices are made. The altar is the place where we meet with God. The altar is the place where we minister unto God and the altar is where God has placed His name.

The Altar
Remember, we have established from the word that the altar is where God has placed his name. So

there is a place in you that bears the name of God. There is a part of you that is God's namesake. Let us look into His word.

'God is a Spirit: and they that worship him must worship him in spirit and in truth.'

John 4:24 KJV

God, the maker of man, is a spirit. A man is made up of the body, soul and spirit. The altar of a man is where God's name is, this is where God's resemblance is. ***Therefore the spirit of a man is the altar of the man.***

UNDERSTANDING THE CONCEPT OF THE ALTAR IN A MAN

When God wants to reach out to a man, he reaches out to the spirit of the man.

'The spirit of man is the candle of the Lord, Searching all the inward parts of the belly.'

Proverbs 20:27 KJV

This simple analogy will help explain how God dwells in us by His Spirit.

Let us use a telecommunication company to explain this better. We have a number of them here in Nigeria, West Africa.

Using MTN, for example, you would agree with me that a man cannot possibly lift up MTN Nigeria as a physical building and put it in his pocket as he goes about his daily activities.

But he can purchase an MTN SIM card that carries the fullness of the entire company. When the man buys an MTN SIM card and inserts it into his phone, he has the fullness of the company with him without having to carry the physical building.

The spirit of man is like the SIM port inside the phone. The SIM card represents the Holy Ghost. The fullness of God is decoded inside the Holy Ghost that comes inside a man by dwelling in the spirit of that man. The man carries God by the spirit. Do you have God inside you? Yes! How? By the spirit!

How can the God who created the heavens and the earth live inside a man? Yes, it is possible, by the spirit. The telecommunication company is big but their SIM card is small. The small SIM card carries the fullness of the company. Everything the company represents is inside the SIM card. The greatness of God is decoded inside the Holy Ghost.

'Know ye not that ye are the temple of God, and that the Spirit of God dwelleth in you?'

1 Corinthians 3:16 KJV

You are the temple of God. God dwells in you by the spirit. The spirit of man is the altar and the Holy Ghost dwells in the spirit of man.

'And he that keepeth his commandments dwelleth in him, and he in him. And hereby we know that he abideth in us, by the Spirit which he hath given us.
'

1 John 3:24 KJV

From the scripture above, it is clear that God dwells in you by His spirit.

'The Spirit itself beareth witness with our spirit, that we are the children of God:'

Romans 8:16 KJV

'That which is born of the flesh is flesh; and that which is born of the Spirit is spirit. '

John 3:6 KJV

You are a child of God by the spirit. By the Holy Spirit, you know who you are. You are a child of God by the Holy Spirit which is an embodiment of God inside of you. You are known as a child of God by the spirit.

What makes your altar an altar as a man is not that you have a spirit but that you have the Holy Spirit inside your spirit.

What makes your altar the altar that God can access is that His name is on the altar. Remember, your body is the sacrifice that should be on the altar.

WHAT HAPPENS ON THE ALTAR?

'And the fire upon the altar shall be burning in it; it shall not be put out: and the priest shall burn wood on it every morning, and lay the burnt offering in order upon it; and he shall burn thereon the fat of the peace offerings. The fire shall ever be burning upon the altar; it shall never go out.'

Leviticus 6:12-13 KJV

The priest is to burn the wood on the altar every morning. He is also to ensure that there is sacrifice on the altar.

The purpose of the wood is to keep the fire burning. The wood is fuel and the reason why we add fuel to anything is to ensure the fire doesn't stop burning.

We also have to consider the fact that nobody

wastes fuel for nothing. Fuel is actually added because of the sacrifice on the altar so that the sacrifice can burn continually.

There is a command to the priest to ensure that the fire must never go out. Thinking about this scripture now, we see that the activities on the altar are serious.

The priest has a duty of ensuring that there is sacrifice on the altar, and a constant supply of wood to ensure that the fire burning the sacrifice on the altar must not go out.

IN THE PREVIOUS CHAPTER, WE HAVE ESTABLISHED THAT:

You are the priest
Your body is the sacrifice
Your spirit is the altar
Your soul is your will to ensure that the task is effectively carried out

The wood is the word, prayers, meditation, fellowship with other brethren, consecration and so on.

This whole process means that you must sacrifice your body on the altar of the spirit by walking in the spirit and mortifying (killing) the works of the flesh. This can only be done by the spirit

'For if ye live after the flesh, ye shall die: but if ye through the Spirit do mortify the deeds of the body, ye shall live.'

Romans 8:13 KJV

You as the priest must ensure that the fuel (wood) is constantly added to ensure that the fire that is killing the deeds of the flesh doesn't go out. The following scriptures illustrate my previous explanations:

'This I say then, Walk in the Spirit, and ye shall not fulfil the lust of the flesh. For the flesh lusteth against the Spirit, and the Spirit against the flesh: and these are contrary the one to the other: so that ye cannot do the things that ye would. '

Galatians 5:16-17 KJV

A believer that starts listening to the world, stops praying, stops fellowshipping with the brethren will in a matter of time return back to the things of the flesh.

So there must be a consistent adding of the wood. For instance, the more we hear the word, the more our conduct changes because we are doing the word and the word is shaping us into the image of Christ.

HOW TO MAINTAIN THE FIRE ON YOUR ALTAR?

Being on fire is not as important as maintaining the fire. We have heard the stories of folks who used to be on fire for the Lord, passionate for the things of the kingdom, full of vigour, energy, and vision.

They were at the forefront of evangelism, missions, discipleship but later in life, they became a shadow of who they used to be.

Some of the folks who were at the forefront of the move of God on campus are nowhere to be found now when it pertains to the issues of the kingdom. No wonder the preacher said this in the book of Ecclesiastes:

'I have observed something else under the sun. The fastest runner doesn't always win the race, and the strongest warrior doesn't always win the

battle. The wise sometimes go hungry, and the skillful are not necessarily wealthy. And those who are educated don't always lead successful lives. It is all decided by chance, by being in the right place at the right time.'

Ecclesiastes 9:11 NLT

We have seen the first become last and the last become first.

'But many that are first shall be last; and the last shall be first.'

Matthew 19:30 KJV

Therefore, carrying the fire is not enough. You have to maintain the fire and fan it into flames consistently. That's the main thing.

HOW DO YOU MAINTAIN THE FIRE ON THE ALTAR AND HOW DO YOU FAN IT INTO FLAMES?

You first need an understanding of the source of the fire. Where is the source of the fire?

Jesus is the baptizer with fire. No man can create

fire by himself. At salvation, there is a deposit of God's fire in the heart of a new creation.

This fire represents the love of God, passion for the things of the kingdom, hunger and thirst, excitement for kingdom things, enthusiasm, doggedness, the desire to know God, service, the heart for evangelism and the desire to please God.

'I indeed baptize you with water unto repentance: but he that cometh after me is mightier than I, whose shoes I am not worthy to bear: he shall baptize you with the Holy Ghost, and with fire:'

Matthew 3:11 KJV

Fire is what is planted into the heart of anyone who accepts Jesus as his Lord and Savior.

Fire can also be described as the power to do God's work with fervency and energy. The fire is given by Jesus but the work of the believer, who is the priest, is to ensure that the fire on his altar doesn't go out.

Therefore, there are certain things you should do to ensure the fire keeps burning. These things are not necessarily big things but small things done over and over again. Consistency is the secret to maintaining a burning life.

Your spirit must be aglow for the Lord every minute. To maintain an altar of fire, certain disciplines must be done daily.

THE FOLLOWING ARE WAYS TO MAINTAIN THE FIRE ON YOUR ALTAR:

A LIFE OF DEVOTION:
I know a lady who was motivated by another lady's weight loss testimony. She was so inspired that she told herself she was going to achieve the same result. She set up a strict diet and exercise/fitness routine to be achieved on a daily basis. She was bent on losing weight no matter what.

She got a fitness coach and followed all the laid down rules strictly. Against all odds, she pursued her goal, ignored all the delicacies she loved just so she could achieve her goal.

Eventually, she achieved her aim, lost several calories and became fit and strong. Her success story was possible because of her devotion and commitment to a daily life of routine.

As believers, we also need to shed some excess spiritual weights just like ***Hebrews 12:1 KJV says: 'Wherefore seeing we also are compassed about with so great a cloud of witnesses, let us lay aside every weight, and the sin which doth so easily beset us, and let us run with patience the race that is set before us, '***

This cannot be done via a singular activity. It has to be done via a commitment to a life of daily routine. A life of devotion is your pathway to a robust and rich personal relationship with God.

The first thing the devil is interested in and in turn wants to attack in your life is not your money, position or title. It's your fellowship with the Lord. He wants to crumble the time you spend with God.

He wants to make you feel or think that you are busy and that you have other more important issues to attend to that are far more important than the time you spend in God's presence on a daily basis.

He is not moved by your once in a while activity. But as soon as he starts seeing a sense of devotion and commitment, he becomes threatened. The farther a man is from his maker the happier the devil is.

A life of devotion is critical to maintaining the fire on the altar.

These are some enemies of a devoted life:

- Misplaced priorities
- Distractions
- Excuses of religious activities
- Lack of wisdom for time management
- Need-centred Christianity – only seeking God when there is a need.

FEED ON THE DIET OF THE SPIRIT CONSISTENTLY- the word of God: You must spend quality time with the word of God daily. Your devotion to God's word should be more than your devotion to social media.

Jeremiah 23:29a KJV   Is not my word like as a fire? Saith the Lord;

The word is fire. When you feed on fire you become fire. The more you feed, the more the fire increases.

'Thy words were found, and I did eat them; and thy word was unto me the joy and rejoicing of mine heart: for I am called by thy name, O Lord God of hosts.'

Jeremiah 15:16 KJV

The word of God is eatable.

'But he answered and said, It is written, Man shall not live by bread alone, but by every word that proceedeth out of the mouth of God.'

Matthew 4:4 KJV

The word of God is food for man. The more you eat, the more you grow.

'It is the spirit that quickeneth; the flesh profiteth nothing: the words that I speak unto you, they are spirit, and they are life.'

John 6:63 KJV

The word of God is spirit and life. Eat the word and live. The fire of a man who feeds on the word never dies, it grows.

'And be not drunk with wine, wherein is excess; but be filled with the Spirit; speaking to yourselves in psalms and hymns and spiritual songs, singing and making melody in your heart to the Lord;'

Ephesians 5:18-19 KJV

The word of God is a drink.

Praying (especially praying in the Holy Ghost):

'But you, beloved, build yourselves up on [the foundation of] your most holy faith [continually progress, rise like an edifice higher and higher], pray in the Holy Spirit,'

Jude 1:20 AMP

The more you pray in the Holy Ghost, the more you rise. The more you pray in the spirit, the more you make progress in life. The more your altar is strengthened and renewed to burn.

'And be not drunk with wine, wherein is excess; but be filled with the Spirit;'

Ephesians 5:18 KJV

A man cannot be drunk and it will not show. You can't spend quality time praying in the Holy Ghost and not burn!

Nobody gets drunk by smelling wine. Everyone who gets drunk gets drunk by drinking, and not just one bottle but many bottles. It's the same way in the spirit. The secret of getting drunk in the Holy Ghost is by spending quality time in God's presence praying, fellowshipping and staying in koinonia with the Holy Ghost.

'Confess to one another, therefore, your faults (your slips, your false steps, your offenses, your sins) and pray [also] for one another, that you may be healed and restored [to a spiritual tone of mind and heart]. The earnest (heartfelt, continued) prayer of a righteous man makes tremendous power available [dynamic in its working].'

James 5:16 AMPC

The strategy for making power available is prayers. Until a man begins to pray, power (fire) is not released or made available. To increase power(fire) is to increase prayers.

'Pray without ceasing.'

1 Thessalonians 5:17 KJV

The more you do it, the more empowered you become. Speak to God in the language of the Spirit. A spirit should speak the language of the spirit.

'Ye know that ye were Gentiles, carried away unto these dumb idols, even as ye were led.'

1 Corinthians 12:2 KJV
This is the language of zion.

Meditation – thinking and meditating on the things of God; setting your mind on things above.

'My heart was hot within me, while I was musing the fire burned: Then spake I with my tongue.'

Psalm 39:3 KJV

When you think about something consistently, you will begin to attract what you are thinking about. The scriptures made it clear in Proverbs 23:7 that as a man thinks in his heart so is he. Think fire and become fire, think increase and have more!

If you can think it, then you can have it. Meditation simply means thinking through scriptures, asking questions, comparing scripture with scripture.

'Now unto him that is able to do exceeding abundantly above all that we ask or think, according to the power that worketh in us, '

Ephesians 3:20 KJV

'This book of the law shall not depart out of thy mouth; but thou shalt meditate therein day and night, that thou mayest observe to do according to all that is written therein: for then thou shalt make thy way prosperous, and then thou shalt have good success. '

Joshua 1:8 KJV

Meditate on the kingdom, meditate on God's power and you will have it.

Hunger and thirst for more of God.

'As the hart panteth after the water brooks, So panteth my soul after thee, O God. My soul thirsteth for God, for the living God: When shall I come and appear before God?'
Psalm 42:1-2

Hunger and thirst are the keys to having more of God. God is the God of power and fire. The more of Him you desire, the more space you create in your life for Him.

The more room you create in your life for Him, the more He occupies you with His fullness. Genuine hunger comes with a panting, a yearning, a longing and a desire for more of God.

'O God, thou art My God; early will I seek thee: My soul thirsteth for thee, my flesh longeth for thee In a dry and thirsty land, where no water is; To see thy power and thy glory, So as I have seen thee in the sanctuary. '

Psalm 63:1-2 KJV

Spiritual hunger comes with a heightened passion to know God more, to be used by Him. Just like the way the stomach growls for food when hungry, so the spirit of a man longs for more of God. Nothing else can satisfy him until He has found God.

As your appetite for God increases, little things will no longer satisfy you. Your bowels will become enlarged. What used to excite you before suddenly stops exciting you because of your desire for more.

Only those who hunger and thirst shall be filled. Your prayer life is proof of your diet and appetite for God. If you are really hungry for more of God, you will pray, you will spend more time with Him, you will want to please Him.

When a man begins to hunger and thirst after God, He already has an invitation to receive from God. Only the hungry and thirsty are capable of receiving.

' Blessed are they which do hunger and thirst after righteousness: for they shall be filled.

Matthew 5:6 KJV

'In the last day, that great day of the feast, Jesus

stood and cried, saying, If any man thirst, let him come unto me, and drink. He that believeth on me, as the scripture hath said, out of his belly shall flow rivers of living water. '

John 7:37-38 KJV

'Ho, every one that thirsteth, come ye to the waters, and he that hath no money; come ye, buy, and eat; yea, come, buy wine and milk without money and without price. Wherefore do ye spend money for that which is not bread? and your labour for that which satisfieth not? hearken diligently unto me, and eat ye that which is good, and let your soul delight itself in fatness. '

Isaiah 55:1-2 KJV

'And the Spirit and the bride say, Come. And let him that heareth say, Come. And let him that is athirst come. And whosoever will, let him take the water of life freely. '

Revelation 22:17 KJV

HOW TO BLOW UP YOUR FIRE

It is important that the fire on your altar is maintained, but your fire can only burn to its capacity. The fire that will consume a log of wood cannot be compared to the fire that will consume a forest.

Fire has levels. It is important that your fire is maintained, but guess what? It is more important for you to blow up that fire!

Remember your duty as a priest. You are to gather up and add wood to your altar so that the fire does not go out and the sacrifice keeps burning.

If your wood will catch fire and burn, then there is a need for you to blow it up.

HOW THEN CAN YOU BLOW UP YOUR FIRE?

Consecration:
Consecration is the setting apart for the king's business. This is being separated from the works of the flesh and living in holiness and sanctification. Men who matter in the things of God are consecrated men.

'Nevertheless the foundation of God standeth sure, having this seal, The Lord knoweth them that are his. And, Let every one that nameth the name of Christ depart from iniquity.

But in a great house there are not only vessels of gold and of silver, but also of wood and of earth; and some to honour, and some to dishonour. If a man therefore purge himself from these, he shall be a vessel unto honour, sanctified, and meet for the master's use, and prepared unto every good work.

Flee also youthful lusts: but follow righteousness, faith, charity, peace, with them that call on the Lord out of a pure heart. '

2 Timothy 2:19-22 KJV

Anyone that will carry authentic fire and fresh mantle will be a man that has purged himself of youthful lust. You can't be living in immorality and say that you are carrying fire. Consecration is the roasting of the body on the altar.

'Thou hast loved righteousness, and hated iniquity; Therefore God, even thy God, hath anointed thee With the oil of gladness above thy fellows. '

Hebrews 1:9 KJV

The anointing came as a result of loving righteousness and hating iniquity.

God can do mighty things through a yielded vessel. This is why He commanded us to live holy lives.

'As obedient children, not fashioning yourselves according to the former lusts in your ignorance: but as he which hath called you is holy, so be ye holy in all manner of conversation; because it is written, Be ye holy; for I am holy. '

1 Peter 1:14-16 KJV

Worship:

After maintaining the good standard of an ideal altar, spice up your sacrifice with quality worship unto the Lord. We were created for worship. As we begin to worship God in spirit and in truth, we begin to experience an increase on all sides. Fresh fire is released.

'God is a Spirit: and they that worship him must worship him in spirit and in truth. '

John 4:24 KJV

Impartation:

Your fire can be blown up and increased by reason of impartation. Impartation here is the sharing and the pouring out of a higher entity into another (usually lower) entity.

As a result, the latter begins to function and operate in the same dimension as the former.

'For I long to see you, that I may impart unto you some spiritual gift, to the end ye may be established;'

Romans 1:11 KJV

You can be imparted with the dimension of fire you desire by the laying on of hands.

'Neglect not the gift that is in thee, which was given thee by prophecy, with the laying on of the hands of the presbytery. "

1 Timothy 4:14 KJV

Impartation will shift, move and put you forward. Impartation is the divine assistance for your elevation.

God bless you!

THE EXPECTATION OF JESUS

The expectation of Jesus for us is that we are blazing and burning for Him. Our altar must be on fire consistently. We are not expected to be cold. We are to mortify the works of the flesh, flee youthful lust and anything that might stop our fire from burning continually.

The fire in the life of a believer is one of the main focuses of Jesus. Jesus is interested in a burning believer because He is the one that baptizes with fire.

"Those who repent I baptize with water, but there is coming a man after me who is more powerful than I. In fact, I'm not even worthy enough to pick up his sandals. He will submerge you into union with the Spirit of Holiness and with a raging fire!"

Matthew 3:11 TPT

"I have come to set the earth on fire, and how I wish it were already ablaze with fiery passion for God!

Luke 12:49 TPT

SOME PROOF THAT A MAN IS ON FIRE

A BOILING LOVE FOR GOD

You are to love the Lord Yahweh, your God, with every passion of your heart, with all the energy of your being, with every thought that is within you, and with all your strength. This is the great and supreme commandment.

Mark 12:30 TPT

Fiery passion for God and the activities of the kingdom

For the zeal of thine house hath eaten me up; and the reproaches of them that reproached thee are fallen upon me.

Psalms 69:9 KJV

GLOWING ENTHUSIASM AND EXCITEMENT:

When a man is on fire, there is an excitement about spiritual things that overwhelm such an individual.

Be enthusiastic to serve the Lord, keeping your passion toward him boiling hot! Radiate with the glow of the Holy Spirit and let him fill you with excitement as you serve him.

Romans 12:11 TPT

AGGRESSIVE EVANGELISM:

A man on fire will be loud about Jesus and the kingdom. He won't be able to keep quiet. He would want everyone to know about the Lord. He will always be on the lookout for opportunities to share the gospel.

If I say, "I will not remember Him Or speak His name anymore," Then my heart becomes a burning fire Shut up in my bones. And I am weary of enduring and holding it in; I cannot endure it [nor contain it any longer]. Jeremiah 20:9 AMP

When a man is on fire, he cannot contain it. It's like there is about to be an explosion inside his heart. He will want to let out what he has on his inside. Hunger and thirst for more of God with a strong desperation

My soul followeth hard after thee: thy right hand upholdeth me. Psalm 63:8 KJV

Hunger and thirst are major prerequisites in receiving from God. Only the hungry are qualified to receive from God. Invitations for spiritual elevation and advancement are only for the hungry and thirsty.

"On the last day, that great day of the feast, Jesus stood and cried out, saying, "If anyone thirsts, let him come to Me and drink. He who believes in Me, as the Scripture has said, out of his heart will flow rivers of living water."

But this He spoke concerning the Spirit, whom those believing in Him would receive; for the Holy Spirit was not yet given, because Jesus was not yet glorified."

John 7:37-38 NKJV

STRONG PRAYER LIFE AND DILIGENT WORD STUDY LIFE

"But we will give ourselves continually to prayer and to the ministry of the word."

Acts 6:4 NKJV

A man with a blazing altar will always yearn for God's word and will always desire to spend quality time with God in the place of prayers.

Prayer and the study of God's word are not something we are to be doing once in a while or occasionally. It is supposed to be a daily concurrence, a daily routine.

Then He spoke a parable to them, that men always ought to pray and not lose heart,

Luke 18:1 NKJV

But He answered and said, "It is written, 'Man shall not live by bread alone, but by every word that proceeds from the mouth of God.' "

Matthew 4:4 NKJV

We are to live by the word and prayers,

STRONG LOVE AND DESIRE FOR THE HOUSE OF GOD.

Anyone on fire for God will always love the house of God. They will always be eager to be in God's presence, attend meetings, conferences, conventions and retreats that will draw them closer to God and empower them more for service.

One thing have I desired of the Lord, that will I seek after; that I may dwell in the house of the Lord all the days of my life, to behold the beauty of the Lord, and to enquire in his temple. Psalms 27:4 (NKJV)

OPERATING IN THE SUPERNATURAL AND MANIFESTING THE GIFTS OF THE SPIRIT

The expectation of Jesus is that the believer will be operating in signs and wonders.

I believe Jesus will be shocked or he is shocked when he sees believers not operating in the supernatural. We are already empowered to do mighty things.

"Most assuredly, I say to you, he who believes in Me, the works that I do he will do also; and greater works than these he will do, because I go to My Father.

John 14:12 NKJV

And these signs will follow those who believe: In My name they will cast out demons; they will speak with new tongues; they will take up serpents; and if they drink anything deadly, it will by no means hurt them; they will lay hands on the sick, and they will recover." Mark 16:17-18 NKJV

All believers have a mandate to operate in the supernatural. The supernatural is our DNA. We are not supposed to live less.

The Holy Ghost is given to us as another comforter and one of the roles of the Holy Ghost is to release power.

And the purpose of this power is so we can be witnesses of the resurrection and power of Jesus. And there is no witnessing without miracles, signs and wonder.

"But you shall receive power when the Holy Spirit has come upon you; and you shall be witnesses to Me in Jerusalem, and in all Judea and Samaria, and to the end of the earth."

Acts 1:8 NKJV

If we also have the Holy Ghost, we are to operate in the gifts of the Holy Ghost. They are gifts. Our work is to receive the gifts and begin to manifest them.

"But the manifestation of the Spirit is given to each one for the profit of all: for to one is given the word of wisdom through the Spirit, to another the word of knowledge through the same Spirit, to another faith by the same Spirit, to another gifts of healings by the same Spirit, to another the working of miracles, to another prophecy, to another discerning of spirits, to another different kinds of tongues, to another the interpretation of tongues. But one and the same Spirit works all these things, distributing to each one individually as He wills."

I Corinthians 12:7-11 NKJV

CLASSIFICATION AND DEFINITION OF GIFTS

Gifts fall into three natural divisions. They are as follows:

GIFTS OF REVELATION - THE MIND GIFTS:

The word of wisdom: This is the supernatural revelation or insight into the divine will and purpose of God showing how to solve any problem that may arise.

Jesus said to her, "Go, call your husband, and come here." The woman answered and said, "I have no husband." Jesus said to her, "You have well said, 'I have no husband,' for you have had five husbands, and the one whom you now have is not your husband; in that you spoke truly." The woman said to Him, "Sir, I perceive that You are a prophet.

John 4:16-19 NKJV

THE WORD OF KNOWLEDGE:

This is the supernatural revelation of divine knowledge, or insights into the divine mind, will, or plans of God and also the plans of others that men cannot know by themselves.

"But Peter said, "Ananias, why has Satan filled your heart to lie to the Holy Spirit and keep back part of the price of the land for yourself? While it remained, was it not your own? And after it was sold, was it not in your own control? Why have you conceived this thing in your heart? You have not lied to men but to God."

Acts 5:3 NKJV

DISCERNING OF SPIRITS:

This is the supernatural revelation or insight into the realm of spirits to detect them, their plans and to read the minds of people.

Then Saul, who also is called Paul, filled with the Holy Spirit, looked intently at him and said, "O full of all deceit and all fraud, you son of the devil, you enemy of all righteousness, will you not cease perverting the straight ways of the Lord?

Acts 13:9-10 NKJV

2. GIFTS OF INSPIRATION-VOCAL GIFTS:

The gift of prophecy: This is a supernatural utterance in the native tongue. It is a miracle of divine utterance, not conceived by human thought or reasoning. It includes speaking to people unto edification, exhortation and comfort.

Then one of them, named Agabus, stood up and showed by the Spirit that there was going to be a great famine throughout all the world, which also happened in the days of Claudius Caesar.

Acts 11:28 NKJV

Divers kinds of tongues: This is a supernatural utterance in other languages which are not known to the speaker.

"And they were all filled with the Holy Spirit and began to speak with other tongues, as the Spirit gave them utterance. And there were dwelling in Jerusalem Jews, devout men, from every nation under heaven. And when this sound occurred, the multitude came together, and were confused, because everyone heard them speak in his own language.

Then they were all amazed and marveled, saying to one another, "Look, are not all these who speak Galileans? And how is it that we hear, each in our own language in which we were born?

Parthians and Medes and Elamites, those dwelling in Mesopotamia, Judea and Cappadocia, Pontus and Asia, Phrygia and Pamphylia, Egypt and the parts of Libya adjoining Cyrene, visitors from Rome, both Jews and proselytes, Cretans and Arabs—we hear them speaking in our own tongues the wonderful works of God."

Acts 2:4-11 NKJV

THE INTERPRETATION OF TONGUES:

This is simply the supernatural ability to interpret in the native tongue what is uttered in other languages not known by the one who interprets by the Spirit.

Therefore let him who speaks in a tongue pray that he may interpret. For if I pray in a tongue, my spirit prays, but my understanding is unfruitful. What is the conclusion then?

I will pray with the spirit, and I will also pray with the understanding. I will sing with the spirit, and I will also sing with the understanding.

I Corinthians 14:13-15 NKJV

3. POWER-WORKING GIFTS:

THE GIFT OF FAITH: This is the supernatural ability to believe God beyond human doubt, unbelief, and reasoning.

"So Jesus said to them, "Because of your unbelief; for assuredly, I say to you, if you have faith as a mustard seed, you will say to this mountain, 'Move from here to there,' and it will move; and nothing will be impossible for you."

Matthew 17:20 NKJV

THE GIFT OF HEALING: This is the supernatural power to heal all manner of sickness without human aid or medicine.

"they will take up serpents; and if they drink anything deadly, it will by no means hurt them; they will lay hands on the sick, and they will recover."

Mark 16:18 NKJV

THE GIFT OF THE WORKING OF MIRACLES:

This is the supernatural power to intervene in the ordinary course of nature and to counteract natural laws if necessary.

"Most assuredly, I say to you, he who believes in Me, the works that I do he will do also; and greater works than these he will do, because I go to My Father."

John 14:12 NKJV

The expectation of Jesus is that we are taking advantage of these gifts and manifesting them to glorify God and destroy the works of darkness anywhere and everywhere we find them.

We can also covet what we don't have but see in the lives of other believers.

But earnestly desire the best gifts. And yet I show you a more excellent way.

I Corinthians 12:31 NKJV

www.ingramcontent.com/pod-product-compliance
Lightning Source LLC
Chambersburg PA
CBHW061259140726
47998CB00006B/2294